Teacher Created Materials

Editor
Mara Ellen Guckian

Managing Editor
Ina Massler Levin, M.A.

Editor-in-Chief
Sharon Coan, M.S. Ed.

Art Director
CJae Froshay

Art Coordinator
Kevin Barnes

Cover Artist
Barb Lorseyedi

Imaging
Alfred Lau
Temo Parra

Product Manager
Phil Garcia

Publishers
Rachelle Cracchiolo, M.S. Ed.
Mary Dupuy Smith, M.S. Ed.

Belair

Editor
Helen Banbury

Layout Artist
Suzanne Ward

Original Cover Design
Ed Gallagher

Illustrations
Catherine Ward,
 Simon Girling Associates
Kristy Wilson,
 Graham-Cameron Illustrations

Authors

Steve Harrison and Patricia Harrison

This edition is published by arrangement with © Folens Limited.

First Published © 1999 Belair Publications

Every effort has been made to contact copyright holders of material used in this book. If any have been overlooked, we will be pleased to make any necessary arrangements.

Teacher Created Materials, Inc.
6421 Industry Way
Westminster, CA 92683
www.teachercreated.com
ISBN-0-7439-3263-3
©2002 Teacher Created Materials, Inc.
Reprinted, 2002
Made in U.S.A.

Table of Contents

Table of Contents

Introduction

The use of writing prompts and models (frames) has been shown to assist many children in the structuring of their writing. Children who lack confidence in their writing find such support extremely helpful. Many models or frames currently in use in schools are generic, such as explanations, reports, investigations, and comparison charts. While you will find these are included in *Writing Prompts and Models,* you will find the concept of writing frames has been taken a step further. This new generation of writing frames is linked closely to not only the process of writing, but also the curriculum content that provides the context for much of the writing children will do in class.

Versions of the nursery rhymes, fairy tales and counting rhymes which serve as focal points for many of the prompts have been provided for you at the beginning of the book. Other frames on the disk can be edited to accommodate materials currently being used in the classroom. Still other frames are generic and can be used repeatedly with different subject matter.

Using the Prompts and Models

A key purpose of writing models (frames) is to develop high quality writing. Children should know they are expected to write in full sentences that are correctly punctuated and written legibly. Many reproducible pages in the past have required single word responses. The frames included here require a broader range of responses, including coherent prose.

The options available through the use of disks mean that work can be tailored to the specific needs of individual pupils. Students can be challenged to produce high quality, extended writing across the curriculum. Students with learning differences can have frames modified to provide support for their particular needs in developing and improving their literacy skills. The "expandable" nature of the frames on disk allows students of all levels to work independently, developing self-esteem as they improve their writing skills and as the information they are able to add to their frames grows.

Introduction (cont.)

Writing Frames on Disks

You will find two formats for these writing frames: on paper and on disk. The disks offer enormous opportunities for both teachers and children. Key features include:

- Frames on disk can be altered. If you, as a teacher, want to modify the number of boxes or the text starters in any frame, you can do so easily. This allows you to tailor the work more specifically to the needs of your class or to individuals within it. You can simplify text; add complexity to the language and structure; create cloze activities; or provide various options as answers, to be deleted to leave the correct answer.

- Paper-based frames are inflexible. They impose limits on how much children can write. The disks have no such limits. The text will simply scroll on and the frame, in effect, expands to accommodate whatever the child wants to write.

- At the "print-out" stage the boxes disappear. The child prints out a page of continuous text. No one can see what part was provided in advance (prompt questions) and what part the child added (answers to the prompts). However, those pages with pictures and tables retain the boxes and print out a "screen shot" of all the elements on the screen.

- The disks can allow pictures and diagrams to be inserted into the frames, ready for printing (see the Help file on the disk for instructions).

- The disks also contain subject-specific vocabulary. Children who need a word can check the vocabulary list and paste that word into their text. You or the children can add words to this vocabulary list, as appropriate.

- Finally, you can modify the frames on-screen and then print them out for children to use as paper frames.

System Requirements

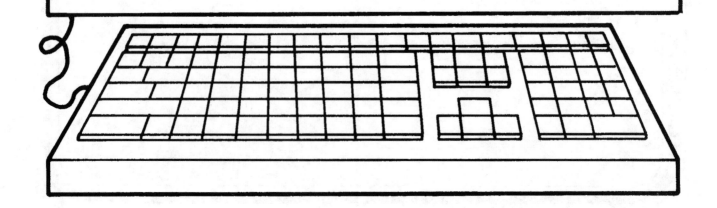

Windows

200 MHz Intel Pentium Processor or greater

Windows 95, 98, NT4, 2000

32MB or more of available RAM

100 MB of available disk space

CD-ROM drive

256-color monitor capable of 800 x 600 resolution

Macintosh

180 MHz PowerPC

MAC OS 8.1 or later

32 MB or more of available RAM

100 MB of available disk space

CD-ROM drive

256-color monitor capable of 800 x 600 resolution

Rhymes

Mary Had a Little Lamb

Mary had a little lamb,
Its fleece was white as snow;
And everywhere that Mary went
The lamb was sure to go.
It followed her to school one day.
Which was against the rule.
It made the children laugh and play,
To see a lamb at school.

Little Bo Peep

Little Bo Peep
Has lost her sheep,
And doesn't know where
To find them.
Leave them alone,
And they'll come home
Wagging their tails
Behind them.

Little Jack Horner

Little Jack Horner
Sat in a corner,
Eating a Christmas pie.
He put in his thumb,
And pulled out a plum,
And said,
"What a good boy am I!"

Jack and Jill

Jack and Jill
Went up a hill,
To fetch a pail of water.
Jack fell down,
And broke his crown,
And Jill came tumbling after.

Rhymes (cont.)

Little Miss Muffet

Little Miss Muffet
Sat on a tuffet
Eating her curds and whey.
Along came a spider
Who sat down beside her
And frightened
Miss Muffet away.

Old Mother Hubbard

Old Mother Hubbard
Went to the cupboard,
To get her poor dog a bone.
But when she got there,
The cupboard was bare,
And so the poor dog had none.

I Caught a Fish Alive

1, 2, 3, 4, 5
I caught a fish alive.
6, 7, 8, 9, 10
I let it go again.
Why did I let it go?
Because it bit my finger so!
Which finger did it bite?
The little finger on the right.

One, Two, Buckle My Shoe

One, two,
buckle my shoe.
Three four,
shut the door.
Five, six,
pick up sticks.
Seven, eight,
close the gate.
Nine, ten,
little red hen.

Fairy Tales

Little Red Riding Hood

Once upon a time a little girl lived with her mother at the edge of the forest. Her grandmother, who lived at the opposite edge of the forest, had made her a red, hooded cloak. She became known as Little Red Riding Hood.

The grandmother was not feeling well, so Little Red Riding Hood's mother baked some cakes for her. Little Red Riding Hood put the cakes in her basket and, wearing her red hood and cloak, set off. Her mother warned her not to talk to strangers.

Not long after she entered the forest she met a wolf. The wolf wanted to gobble her up, but he dared not because there were some woodcutters nearby. Instead, he greeted her politely, saying, "Good morning, Little Red Riding Hood. Where are you going?" Forgetting her mother's warning, the little girl said, "I'm going to my grandmother's."

"And what have you in your basket?" asked the wolf.

"Some cakes. She's not well."

"Oh, I am so sorry," said the wolf. "Where does she live?"

"She lives at the other edge of the forest."

"I see, well…enjoy your walk," said the wolf as he took off through the trees. He knew exactly where he was going. Little Red Riding Hood also continued walking, picking flowers as she went. The big, bad wolf hurried, and in no time he arrived at the grandmother's cottage.

Once there, he knocked on the door: rat-tat-tat-tat.

"Who's there?" said a frail voice from inside.

"It's me, Little Red Riding Hood," pretended the wolf in a high voice. "I've brought you some cakes to help you feel better." Now, the grandmother could tell that it was not really Little Red Riding Hood and she quickly hid.

Meanwhile the wolf, becoming impatient, lifted the latch, opened the door, and crept in. It was dark and he couldn't see very well. When he got to Grandmother's bed she wasn't there. He started to look for her but heard Little Red Riding Hood coming. He quickly put on Grandmother's nightdress, spectacles and nightcap and slid into her bed.

©Teacher Created Materials, Inc.   9   #3263 Writing Prompts and Models

Little Red Riding Hood (cont.)

When Little Red Riding Hood arrived she knocked at the door, just as he had done: rat-tat-tat-tat.

"Who's there?" said the wolf.

"It's me, Little Red Riding Hood. I've brought you some cakes to help you feel better."

The wolf softened his voice and said, "Lift the latch and open the door, my dear."

So Little Red Riding Hood lifted the latch, opened the door and went in.

The wolf had pulled the bedclothes up to his nose, tucked his big ears under the nightcap and peered over the top of Grandmother's spectacles. "Put the cakes on the stool and come visit," he said in a muffled voice.

"Oh Grandmother," she said, "What big ears you have!"

"All the better to hear you with, my dear," said the wolf.

"Oh Grandmother, what big eyes you have!"

"All the better to see you with, my dear."

"Oh Grandmother, what big hands you have!"

"All the better to hold you with, my dear."

"Oh Grandmother, what big teeth you have!"

"All the better to eat you with, my dear."

With that, the wolf sprang out of the bed. Luckily, he got tangled in the bedclothes and Little Red Riding Hood was able to get away. She yelled, knocked over a rocking chair, and ran out the door.

One of the woodcutters was passing by the cottage and heard the terrible commotion. "That's strange," he said to himself. "I wonder if the old grandmother is all right." He opened the cottage door and went over to the bed. He was quite surprised by the mess he found and the large wolf thrashing around in grandmother's clothes. Realizing that the beast must have tried to do harm, he chased him out of the house and deep into the forest.

Then, he rushed back to see Little Red Riding Hood peering into the cottage. "Oh no, where is my poor grandmother?" she said. At that moment, her grandmother scrambled out from under the bed where she had been hiding. She was very scared but the woodcutter and Little Red Riding Hood calmed her down. She ate her cakes and soon felt better.

Finally, Little Red Riding Hood walked home with her friend, the woodcutter. She promised never again to talk to strangers.

10

Fairy Tales *(cont.)*

Jack and the Beanstalk

Once upon a time there was a woman who lived with her son, Jack. When she needed money she sold her things. Soon, all she had left was a cow. She was sorry to sell her cow, but she and Jack needed food. She asked Jack to take the cow to market.

Jack and the cow went off to market. He had not gone far when he met a strange old man. "Where are you taking that cow?" the man asked. "I'm taking her to market," Jack replied. At that, the strange old man reached into his pocket and pulled out a handful of beans of every color. The strange old man told Jack the beans were magical and offered them in exchange for the cow. The silly boy could not resist what seemed to him a bargain. Jack hurried home with the beans to tell his mother the good news. When the poor woman saw the beans, she was very angry. "What? You sold our cow for some miserable beans! Give them to me."

Jack's mother threw the beans out into the garden. Then she sent him to bed without supper. Poor Jack was sad and feeling sorry for himself as he fell asleep. Early the next morning Jack looked out the window and saw that the beans had sprouted. They had twisted and turned forming a giant beanstalk. It was so tall that it vanished into the clouds. Jack was very curious to know what was at the top. He put his foot on the beanstalk and he began to climb: up and up and up. After some time, he reached the top of the beanstalk. He started to walk, and at sunset he came to a big castle. At the door stood a woman as tall as a house.

"Good evening," said Jack politely. "Could you give me a bit of bread? I am very hungry." "What are you doing here?" she answered. "Don't you know that my husband is a giant and you will be his breakfast?" Poor Jack shivered, wishing he was back home. But he was so hungry he didn't move. The wife felt sorry for Jack, so she gave him a great hunk of bread and cheese. He had almost finished eating when, all at once, the castle began to shake. Jack heard very heavy footsteps going thump, thump, thump!

"Quick," said the woman, "hide in the oven." Quick as a flash, Jack jumped into the giant oven and peered out into the kitchen. He saw the giant and heard him roar like thunder. "Fee, fi, fo, fum, I smell a boy!" "Oh, no, my dear," said his wife. "There is no one here but you and I." The giant seemed satisfied and sat down to eat. After, he said to his wife, "Bring me my goose that lays the golden eggs." The woman brought in a goose, and Jack was quite surprised. Every time the giant said "Lay", the goose laid a golden egg. Soon, the giant grew tired and took a nap. His snoring was like the boom-boom of a cannon.

Fairy Tales *(cont.)*

Jack and the Beanstalk *(cont.)*

After a while, Jack crawled out of the oven, grabbed the golden goose, and ran out of the castle. He scrambled down the beanstalk as fast as he could. "Mother," said Jack, "I've brought you a present." He put the goose upon the table and said "Lay". Immediately, the goose laid a golden egg. Jack's mother was amazed and happy. They would not be hungry any more.

After a time, Jack longed to climb the beanstalk again. Despite his mother's warnings, he got up early and again climbed the beanstalk: up and up and up, through the clouds. Making his way to the castle, he saw the woman as tall as a house standing at the door, just as before. He waited till she wasn't looking and ran and hid in the closet. Just then, the castle began to shake, and again he heard, thump, thump, thump! The giant was coming. "Fee, fi, fo, fum, I smell a boy!"

"Oh no, my dear," said his wife. "There is no one here but you and I." The giant seemed content. He ate his supper then called out, "Fetch my bags of gold and silver. I wish to count my money." His wife returned with the money bags. Jack watched as the giant poured the money out. He counted the coins until he fell asleep, snoring like the roar of the ocean. Jack carefully tiptoed from the closet, grabbed the bags, dragged them to the beanstalk, and carried them home.

As time went by Jack wished to try his luck one last time in the giant's castle. Again he put his foot on the beanstalk and began to climb: up and up and up. Again, he crept into the castle when no one was looking and found a hiding place in a giant cooking pot. Soon, the giant returned, thump, thump, thump! "Fee, fi, fo, fum, I smell a boy."

His wife tried to reassure him, but this time he was not convinced. He began to search high and low. Poor Jack was very frightened. Luckily, the giant gave up. When he had finished eating, he shouted out, "Get me the golden harp."

The moment the giant said "Play," the harp played and the giant soon fell into a deep sleep, snoring to the music. That was Jack's chance! He climbed out of the pot, grabbed the harp and started to run. Unfortunately, the moment he picked the harp up, it cried out loudly, "Master, Master, Master!" At once the giant awoke! He stumbled groggily after Jack who ran to the beanstalk and clambered down. As soon as he could see the bottom of the beanstalk he yelled, "Mother, Mother, fetch the axe." By the time he climbed down, his mother was ready. The beanstalk was shaking and swaying under the giant's weight. Jack swung the axe and cut right through the beanstalk. It toppled over and the giant tumbled down. To this day, there is a huge hole where the giant sank out of sight. Jack cared for his mother, and they lived happily for the rest of their days.

Fairy Tales *(cont.)*

The Three Little Pigs

Once upon a time there were three little pigs who lived with their mother. She did not have enough to feed them so she decided to send them out into the world to seek their fortunes.

The first little pig went down the road and after a time met a man with a bundle of straw.

"Good-day, sir," said the little pig. "Will you give me some straw to build a house?"

"Yes, of course, little pig," the kind gentleman replied, and he gave the pig an armful of straw.

The pig chose a good spot and built a straw house. He felt snug and warm inside.

Not long after, a wolf came along. He knocked at the door and called out, "Little pig, little pig, let me in."

"No, no," said the pig. "Not by the hair on my chinny-chin-chin, I won't let you in."

To this the wolf said, "Then I'll huff and I'll puff and I'll blow your house down."

And he did. He huffed and he puffed, and he blew the house down. The first little pig ran away as fast as he could. He didn't look back.

Then, the second little pig said goodbye to his mother and set off to seek his fortune. He had not gone far when he met a man with a bundle of sticks.

"Good-day, sir," said the second little pig. "Will you give me some sticks to build a house?"

"Yes, of course, little pig," the man answered, and he gave the pig an armful of sticks.

Off went the little pig and he built a house of sticks. He lived inside, snug and warm.

Not long after, the wolf came along. He knocked at the door and called out, "Little pig, little pig, let me in."

"No, no," said the pig. "Not by the hair on my chinny-chin-chin, I won't let you in."

And the wolf said, "Then I'll huff and puff and I'll blow your house down."

And he did. He huffed and he puffed, and he puffed and he huffed, and he blew the house down. The second little pig scampered away as fast as he could.

Fairy Tales *(cont.)*

The Three Little Pigs *(cont.)*

Some time later the third little pig was walking down the road when he met a man with a load of bricks.

"Good-day, sir," said the little pig. "Will you give me some bricks to build a house?"

"Yes, of course, little pig," the kind gentleman replied, and he gave the pig a pile of bricks.

Off went the pig and he built a house of bricks. He lived inside, snug and warm.

Later that day the wolf came along, knocked at the door and called out, "Little pig, little pig, let me come in."

"No, no," said the pig. "Not by the hair on my chinny-chin-chin, I won't let you in."

To which the wolf replied, "Then I'll huff and I'll puff and I'll blow your house down."

So he huffed and he puffed, and he puffed and he huffed, and he huffed and he puffed, but he could not blow the house down.

Finally, the wolf grew tired and decided to try to get into the brick house another way. He looked all around the house and then decided to use the chimney. Luckily, the little pig heard him climbing up onto the roof. The little pig had a pot full of water on the fire and it was beginning to bubble. The little pig hurried and added more wood and stoked up the flames.

By the time the wolf got to the chimney, the water below was very hot. The wolf climbed into the chimney and began to slide down. Farther and farther he slid until he got to the bottom. He fell straight into the boiling water. SPLASH! The clever little pig quickly put the lid on the pot and that was the end of the big, bad wolf.

The other two little pigs, who had been hiding in the bushes, were so excited when they saw their brother come out of his house that they squealed. They ran out to greet him in his tiny yard. All three little pigs lived happily in the brick house. They were never bothered by a wolf again.

14

Mary Had a Little Lamb

Helpful Words

fleece
everywhere
snow

Mary _____

Its _____

And _____

_____

It _____

Which was _____

It made _____

_____

Name: _____   Date: _____

Little Bo Peep

Helpful Words

doesn't
sheep
tails

Little _____

_____

And _____

_____

Leave _____

And _____

Wagging _____

_____

Name: _____   Date: _____

Little Jack Horner

Helpful Words

Christmas
corner
plum
thumb

Little _____

Sat _____

Eating _____

He _____

And _____

And said, _____

_____

Name: _____   Date: _____

Jack and Jill

Jack _____

Went _____

To _____

Jack _____

And _____

And Jill _____

Helpful Words

broke   crown   fetch
tumbling   pail

Name: _____   Date: _____

Little Miss Muffet

Little _____

Sat _____

Eating _____

Along _____

And _____

And _____

Helpful Words

curds   spider   tuffet   whey
frightened

Name: _____   Date: _____

Old Mother Hubbard

Old _____

Went _____

To _____

But _____

The _____

And so _____

Helpful Words

bare   bone   cupboard   none

Use this writing frame to write another nursery rhyme with two different characters.

Name: _____   Date: _____

My Favorite Nursery Rhyme

My favorite nursery rhyme is _____

_____

I like this rhyme because _____

_____

_____

_____

_____

The funniest part is when_____

_____

_____

_____

_____

My favorite character is _____

_____

because _____

_____

_____

Name:_____   Date: _____

Jack and the Beanstalk

Jack's mother asks Jack _____

_____

_____

Jack swaps _____

_____

_____

The beanstalk _____

_____

_____

The words the giant says many times are

Name: _____   Date: _____

Little Red Riding Hood

Read the words of
Little Red Riding
Hood and write in
the wolf's reply.

"Grandma, what big eyes you've got."

"All _____

_____"

"Grandma, what a big nose you've got."

"All _____

_____."

"Grandma, what big teeth you've got."

"All _____

_____."

Name: _____   Date: _____

The Three Little Pigs

The first little pig built _____

_____

The second little _____

_____

The third _____

_____

When the wolf stood outside each house, he said, " _____

_____

_____

_____."

The pigs' reply was always, " _____

_____

_____

_____."

Name: _____   Date: _____

My Favorite Fairy Tale

My favorite fairy tale is _____

_____

I like it because _____

_____

_____

_____

My favorite character is _____

_____

because _____

_____

_____

_____

If I could change the ending, I would _____

_____

_____

_____

_____

Name: _____   Date: _____

Fairy Tale Characters

Fairy tales usually have good and bad characters.

Complete the chart and write a sentence about each character.

Fairy Tale	Characters
Sleeping Beauty	Good: Bad:
Snow White and the Seven Dwarfs	Good: Bad:
Rumplestiltskin	Good: Bad:
Jack and the Beanstalk	Good: Bad:

Name: _____ Date: _____

26

Fairy Tale Beginnings

Fairy tales can begin in lots of different ways. Think of a story you know and write three different beginnings.

Helpful Story Beginnings

Once upon a time...   There once was...
Many, many years ago...   Long, long ago...

Name: _____   Date: _____

A Fairy Tale I Know

A fairy tale I know is _____

_____

Once upon a time, _____

_____

_____

_____

Sadly, _____

_____

_____

_____

Happily,_____

_____

_____

_____

Finally,_____

_____

_____

_____

Name:_____   Date: _____

My Own Fairy Tale

The title of my own fairy tale is _____

_____

There are _____characters.

● _____is a _____

who _____

● _____ is a _____

who _____

● _____is a _____

who _____

The main plot of the story is _____

_____

_____

_____

At the end, _____

_____

_____

Name:_____ Date: _____

Counting Rhymes

(I Caught a Fish Alive)

One, two, three, four, five

_____

_____

Six, seven, eight, nine, ten

_____

_____

Why _____

_____

Because _____

_____

Which _____

_____

This _____

_____

Name: _____   Date: _____

30

Counting Rhymes II

(One, Two, Buckle My Shoe)

One, two _____

_____

Three, four _____

_____

Five, six _____

_____

Seven, eight_____

_____

Nine, ten _____

_____

Helpful Words

bricks	door	gate	hen	late
more	new	pen	shoe	sticks

Name: _____   Date: _____

Late for School

Seven in the morning

It's time to stop _____

I'm in a rush

My teeth need a _____

It feels like a race

I must wash _____

Just past the hour

No time for a _____

I'm sure to be late

Better race through the _____

My mom forgot to say,

"Don't you know it's Saturday!"

Name:_____   Date: _____

Parts of Me

Two eyes that I can see with

Two _____

One _____

One _____

One _____

Ten _____

Two _____

Two _____

Two _____

And it all adds up to ME.

Name: _____   Date: _____

Opposites

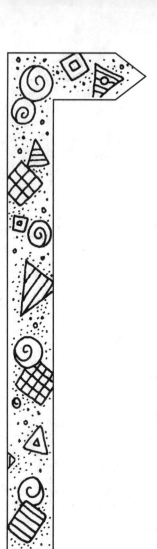

Up, down

Wear a _____

Left, right

Out of _____

In, out

Sing and _____

Under, over

I'm in _____

Flip, flop

Time to _____

Name: _____   Date: _____

Look What I Can Do

Clop, clop

I can _____

Clip, clip

I can _____

Beep, beep

I _____

Ring, ring

_____

Tap, tap

_____

Name:_____   Date: _____

An African Folktale

The best African folktale I know is _____

_____

_____

The folktale is about_____

_____

_____

_____

What I really like in the folktale is when_____

_____

_____

_____

I know it is an African folktale because _____

_____

_____

_____

Name:_____   Date: _____

A Native American Legend

My favorite Native American legend is _____

_____

_____

It takes place in _____

_____

_____

I can tell it is a Native American legend by ____

_____

_____

The main characters are_____

_____

_____

The story makes me feel_____

because _____

_____

_____

_____

Name:_____   Date:_____

Stories About Distant Places

A story I know about a far-away place is_____

_____

The place is_____

_____

The main character is called_____

The story is about_____

_____

_____

_____

_____

The place is different from where I live because

_____

_____

_____

_____

Name:_____ Date:_____

Missing Person

Pinocchio

Pinocchio does not look like other boys because

_____

_____

Pinocchio tells lies.

When he does _____

_____

_____

_____

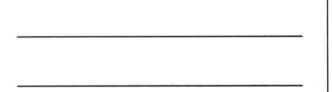

Pinocchio was last seen _____

_____

If you see him, please_____

_____

Name: _____   Date: _____

The Tortoise and the Hare

One day the hare said to _____,

" _____

_____ "

And the moral of the story is_____

_____

Name:_____   Date: _____

My Favorite Character

My favorite character is _____.

_____ is a character in

_____.

_____ is my favorite character

because _____

_____

_____

and _____

_____

The thing I do not like about_____

is _____

_____

If I could change_____

_____

I would _____

_____

Name:_____   Date: _____

Character Behavior

The story I have chosen is _____

_____

The character I will write about is _____

_____, who acted like _____

_____

_____

I think that this behavior was _____

because _____

_____

_____

_____

Another character who behaved like this was

_____ in the story of _____

_____

_____

_____

_____

Name:_____ Date: _____

Character Appearance

The character I have chosen is _____.

_____ is about _____ tall

and weighs _____.

_____'s face is _____ with

_____ hair, _____ eyes, a

_____ mouth, _____ ears

and a _____ nose.

_____ usually wears _____

_____

and _____ on his/her feet.

Sketch of

_____

Name: _____ Date: _____

Wanted

Name _____

Description _____

_____

_____

Last seen _____

_____

_____

Reason_____

_____

_____

Reward _____

_____

_____

Name:_____   Date: _____

Bigger and Bigger

One day the farmer planted _____.

It grew _____ and _____

until _____

So the farmer _____

_____

But _____

_____

_____

Then _____

_____

_____

But still _____

_____

_____

In the end, _____

_____

_____

Name: _____   Date: _____

Tongue Twisters

Some words are difficult to say together.
Say these words as fast as you can.

She sells sea shells on the sea shore.

Choose words which begin with the same letter
to write tongue twisters.

Tim told_____

Mary makes _____

Sam said _____

Nutty Nora _____

Rani rarely_____

Fred fears _____

Now ask a friend to read them fast.
Are they good tongue twisters?

Name:_____   Date: _____

Riddles

What has four wheels and flies?

Answer: A garbage truck

Think of a riddle for these answers.

_____

_____

Answer: sea horse

_____

_____

Answer: daisy chain

_____

_____

Answer: newspaper

_____

_____

Answer: doorbell

Name:_____   Date:_____

My Favorite Poet

My favorite poet is _____

Poems I know are _____

_____

_____

_____

My favorite poem is _____

_____

because _____

_____

_____

_____

A question I would like to ask my favorite poet
is _____

_____

_____

_____

Name: _____   Date: _____

My Favorite Author

My favorite author is _____

_____

Books I know are _____

_____

_____

_____

What I like about the stories is _____

_____

_____

_____

If I met the author, a question I would ask is _____

_____

_____

_____

Name: _____   Date: _____

Fiction or Non-fiction?

Fiction is writing which is not true. Non-fiction is about real people, places and events. Here are some different types of texts you might meet. Check if you think they are fiction or non-fiction.

Text Type	Fiction	Non-fiction
A book about whales		
A fairy tale		
A report on your school Sports Day		
A nursery rhyme		
"The Owl and the Pussycat" poem		
Instructions on how to make a kite		

I like to read fiction when _____

_____

I like to read non-fiction when _____

_____

Name: _____   Date: _____

Parts of Non-fiction Books

The **title** tells me _____

_____

The **contents** is divided into _____

_____

These help me _____

_____

_____

The **index** is at _____

It helps me _____

For example, _____

_____

_____

A **glossary** is useful because _____

_____

_____

Sometimes the back cover has a **blurb**. This __

_____

_____

Name:_____ Date: _____

Non-fiction Books

I like non-fiction books because _____

_____

_____

_____

_____

They help me to _____

_____

_____

Some non-fiction books I have read are _____

_____

_____

_____

_____

If I needed information on _____

_____

I would _____

_____

_____

Name: _____ Date: _____

A Text I Have Read

The text I have read is called_____

_____

This is my plan for writing my own version.

Key words I will use:	Key phrases I will use:

Headings I will use:	Illustrations I will use:

Name:_____   Date:_____

My Topic Glossary

I have been learning about _____

_____

_____

This is my glossary of important words and their meanings.

Words	Meanings

Name: _____ Date: _____

Body Parts

Label the parts of the body.

Name:_____ Date: _____

Shopping Labels

Make up labels to describe the types of food shown below.

Name: _____   Date: _____

56

School Labels

Write the labels for places in school where you would see these:

Name: _____   Date: _____

Things To Do

I am planning _____

_____

Things I need to do are _____

_____

_____

_____

_____

Things others need to do are _____

_____

_____

_____

The most important thing to remember is _____

_____

_____

_____

_____

Name:_____   Date: _____

My Wish List

For _____ I would like:

_____

_____

_____

_____

_____

_____

_____

My favorite _____

_____

and maybe _____

_____

Name:_____   Date: _____

My Vacation List

If I went to _____

during the day I would need _____

_____

_____

_____

I would wear_____

_____

I would like to see _____

_____

_____

_____

At night I would need _____

_____

_____

_____

_____

Name:_____ Date: _____

Giving Directions

To _____

From _____

Turn _____

Walk along until _____

_____

_____

Then, _____

_____

_____

When you reach _____

_____

_____

Finally,_____

_____

_____

_____

_____

Name:_____   Date: _____

Going To. . .

Going to _____

You will need to take _____

_____

_____

_____

When you arrive _____

_____

_____

_____

Don't forget to _____

_____

_____

_____

As you leave _____

_____

_____

_____

Name: _____   Date: _____

How To Make

You will need

First, _____

_____

_____

Next, _____

_____

_____

After that, _____

_____

_____

To finish, _____

_____

Name: _____ Date: _____

A Place I Visited

I went to _____

_____

I went there with _____

_____

_____

_____

We went because _____

_____

_____

_____

When we were there we _____

_____

_____

_____

The best moment was when _____

_____

_____

_____

Name: _____ Date: _____

An Event To Remember

One of the best times I have had was when ___

_____

_____

_____

_____

Other people who were there were _____

_____

_____

The reason it was so good was _____

_____

_____

_____

The best moment was when_____

_____

_____

_____

_____

Name:_____   Date: _____

My Worst Moment

The worst moment of my life was when _____

_____

_____

_____

It all started when _____

_____

_____

And then _____

_____

_____

_____

I cannot forget how _____

_____

_____

_____

If it should happen again, I think I would_____

_____

_____

Name:_____ Date: _____

Postcard

To

Dear _____

I am _____

_____

We are _____

_____

I wish _____

Love _____

Name: _____   Date: _____

Describing an Artifact

The artifact I have chosen is _____

It is made of _____

_____

because _____

_____

Sketch of _____

It is used _____

_____

_____

Normally, it would be used by_____

_____

_____

Name:_____   Date: _____

How To Grow a Healthy Plant

Write captions for each of the pictures.

You will need

_____   _____   _____   _____

First _____

_____

_____

Then _____

_____

_____

Make sure_____

_____

_____

Don't forget _____

_____

_____

Name:_____   Date: _____

How a Bicycle Works

Captions can explain how things work or are used. Write a sentence about each part of this bicycle.

Seat	Handlebars
_____	_____
_____	_____
_____	_____

Pedals	Wheels
_____	_____
_____	_____
_____	_____

Name:_____   Date: _____

Level 1 Non-fiction

How It Works

This is an explanation of how _____

_____ works.

Sketch of _____

Name: _____   Date: _____

©Teacher Created Materials, Inc.   71   #3263 Writing Prompts and Models

Taking a Dog for a Walk

Before you leave home, _____

_____

_____

You need to make sure _____

_____

_____

During the walk, _____

_____

_____

In order to be safe, _____

_____

_____

_____

Whatever happens, don't _____

_____

_____

_____

_____

Name: _____ Date: _____

How I Measure and Record the Temperature

First, I _____

_____

_____

Then, _____

_____

_____

Today's Temperature

Next, _____

_____

_____

Finally, _____

_____

_____

Name: _____ Date: _____

A School Day

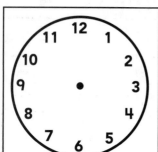

I arrive at school at _____
The first thing I do is _____
_____
_____

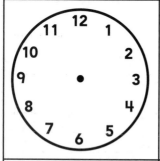

At _____ the class _____
_____
_____
_____

At lunchtime I _____
_____
After that _____
_____

Playtime is _____
I usually _____
_____
_____

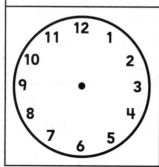

School ends at _____
I go _____
_____
_____

Name: _____   Date: _____

74   ©Teacher Created Materials, Inc.

Weekend

My favorite day is _____

because _____

_____

Morning 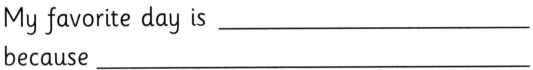 In the morning, I like to _____

_____

_____

_____

_____

Afternoon After lunch, I enjoy _____

_____

I don't enjoy _____

_____

_____

Evening Sometimes in the evening, I ___

_____

_____

_____

I stay up until _____ on weekends.

Name: _____ Date: _____

A Week in the Life of an Adult

The adult I am interviewing is _____

_____

Monday	
Tuesday	
Wednesday	
Thursday	
Friday	
Saturday	
Sunday	

Name: _____   Date: _____

All About Animals

The book I have read is called _____

_____

The author is _____

The book is about _____

_____

_____

_____

_____

The animals it describes include _____

_____

_____

_____

The most interesting animal is _____

because _____

_____

_____

_____

_____

Name: _____   Date: _____

Different Homes

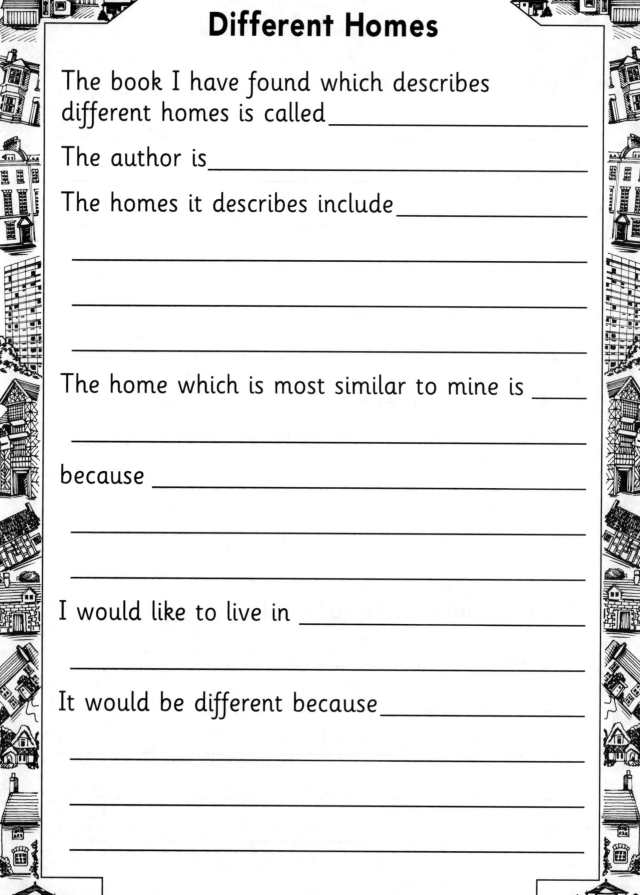

The book I have found which describes different homes is called_____

The author is_____

The homes it describes include_____

_____

_____

_____

The home which is most similar to mine is _____

_____

because _____

_____

_____

I would like to live in _____

_____

It would be different because_____

_____

_____

_____

Name:_____   Date: _____

Vacations

People have vacations because_____

_____

_____

Some people _____

_____

_____

Others _____

_____

_____

I prefer _____

_____

_____

The last vacation I had was with_____

_____

_____

The best part was _____

_____

_____

Name:_____   Date: _____

Jobs People Do

The book I have read about people's jobs is called_____

The author is _____

The contents tells me it is about _____

_____

_____

And _____

_____

The glossary explains new words such as:

Word	Meaning

The index tells_____

_____

Name:_____   Date: _____

All About Me

My name is _____

I am _____ years old.

My hair is _____

and my eyes are _____

My favorite TV programs are_____

_____

_____

_____

My best friends are_____

_____

_____

We play_____

_____

_____

My ideal day would be to _____

_____

_____

_____

Name:_____   Date: _____

What I Want to Learn from this Book

The book I am going to read is called_____

_____

I think it will be about _____

_____

_____

_____

I think this because_____

_____

_____

Questions I want to ask are:

How_____

_____

Why_____

_____

When_____

_____

Who_____

_____

Name:_____   Date:_____

All About You

Ask questions to find out more about someone.

What _____

_____ ?

When _____

_____ ?

Why _____

_____ ?

How _____

_____ ?

Are you _____

_____ ?

Do you _____

_____ ?

Have you ever _____

_____ ?

Name: _____   Date: _____

All About a Place

Write questions to ask someone about a place he or she has visited.

Where _____

_____ ?

When_____

_____ ?

What _____

_____ ?

Was there _____

_____ ?

Did you_____

_____ ?

Were there_____

_____ ?

Will you_____

_____ ?

Name:_____   Date: _____

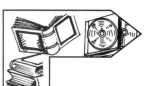

Fiction as a Genre

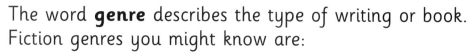

The word **genre** describes the type of writing or book.
Fiction genres you might know are:

adventure/thriller	fantasy	myths
comedy	historical fiction	romance
detective/mystery	horror/ghost	science fiction
diary	humor	soap
fables	legends	tragedy
fairy tales		

Books can cover more than one genre, e.g. historical romance.
Write the genre next to these books.

Book	Genre
James and the Giant Peach	
Goosebumps series	
Star Trek	
Sherlock Holmes	
Little Red Riding Hood	
The Lion, the Witch and the Wardrobe	
Macbeth	

With a partner, try to think of or find books which are
written in the genres on this chart.

Name: _____   Date: _____

Story Plan: Characters

The main character will be called

Appearance

Age:

Height:

Hair:

Distinguishing features will be:

Personality:

Things will happen to her/him, such as

In the end, she/he will

Name: _____   Date: _____

Story Plan: Parallel Plots

Many stories have more than one **plot** or **storyline** going on at any one time.
This is the story I know with more than one plot.

Title:

Storyline 1 is about

The characters involved are

The main event

In conclusion,

Storyline 2 is about

The characters involved are

The main event

In conclusion,

The connection between the two plots is

Name: _____ Date: _____

Story Plan: Familiar Settings

The setting for my story will be

I have chosen this because

I want to develop a sense of

I will do this by making the setting

Other things which will add to the atmosphere of the setting will be

Name: _____   Date: _____

Story Plan: Events

Title:

The first event to happen will be

The key event in the story will be when

The characters involved in this key event will be

As a result,

Eventually,

Name: _____ Date: _____

Story Plan: Structures

Here is an example of a simple story structure:

Title:	Jack and the Beanstalk.
Introduction:	Jack sets off to market to sell the cow for money to buy food.
Problem:	He swaps the cow for magic beans.
Key Event:	He climbs to the top of the beanstalk and encounters the giant.
Conclusion:	Jack kills the giant and takes the giant's gold.

Use this table to plan your own story structure.

Title:

Introduction:

Problem:

Key Event:

Conclusion:

Name: _____ Date: _____

90

Story Plan: Paragraphs

Draft your story. Use notes and key words for your ideas for each paragraph.

Title:

Genre:

Main points in each paragraph:

Paragraphs

1.

2.

3.

4.

Words to help you

| first | second | then | however | but |
| initially | in conclusion | on the other hand |

Name: _____   Date: _____

Story Plan: Overall Plan

Title:

Genre:

My story will be about

The story will start by

Several things will happen, including

The most interesting part will be

I will conclude the story by

Name: _____   Date: _____

92   ©Teacher Created Materials, Inc.

Features of Fairy Tales

I know a story is a fairy tale because

Fairy tales usually have good and wicked characters.
Examples from fairy tales I know are:

Fairy Tale	Good Character	Wicked Character

Fairy tales have similar beginnings. Here are some
beginnings I have read:

In fairy tales, the villain usually carries out a wicked deed.
Examples of two that I know are:

Villain	Wicked deed

Most fairy tales involve a person who saves the day.
Draw a chart like this on the back of this sheet and write
about heros you know in famous fairy tales.

Fairy Tale	Hero	How the problem was solved

Name: _____   Date: _____

Retelling a Fairy Tale

The fairy tale I have chosen to retell is

At the beginning of the story,

The writer kept me interested because

I expected

But I did not expect

In the end,

If I could change the ending, I would

Name: _____   Date: _____

94

Describing Fairy Tale Characters

The fairy tale I have chosen is called

I have chosen this because

The main characters in the story are

They are all different.
                is
                is
                is

My favorite character is
because
The best part of the fairy tale is when

Continue on the back of this sheet.

Name: _____   Date: _____

Points of View in Fairy Tales

People in fairy tales often have different points of view about the same situation.

A story I know where there are different points of view is

The two characters who disagree are
and

thinks

thinks

In the end,

Name: _____   Date: _____

Features of Myths

Myths have some things in common.
They usually have super-human heroes. Here are some I know:

Myth	Hero

Myths usually have monsters and demons. Here are some I know:

Myth	Monster or Demon

Myths are often about the victory of good over evil.
The myth I know best is

Good overcomes evil in this myth by

Name: _____   Date: _____

Creation Stories

Most cultures have stories about how the world began. These are called creation stories. They have features in common:

● They tell what the world was like before people. Describe two more stories you know.

Story	Origin	Description
Adam and Eve	Old Testament	God made the earth in six days and on the seventh, He rested.

● They also explain how people were created.

Describe how this is told in the two stories you know.

In the story of Adam and Eve, God makes Adam and then makes Eve from one of Adam's ribs.

In the story of_____

_____

_____

In the story of_____

_____

_____

● They also tell of how the earth became populated.

On the back of this sheet, write about one of the above stories.

Name:_____ Date:_____

How The World Began

Creation stories explain how the world began.
The myth I know is

The culture this myth comes from is

In the beginning, there was

Then,

After that,

Next,

And since then

Name: _____ Date: _____

The Elements

In the past, people believed there were four elements:

earth

wind

water

fire

Myths often involve one or more of these.
Retell a myth you know which uses the elements.

The myth I have chosen is called

I have chosen this myth because

The elements in the story are

They are used to

I know the story is a myth because

Name: _____   Date: _____

Features of Legends

Legends are stories which could be true. They usually deal with characters from the historical past who are good, honest, and who fight against evil and injustice. These good characters often have a group of companions. Sometimes, the characters they come into contact with have magical or supernatural powers.

The Legend of Robin Hood

Robin Hood's adventures take place during

His main opponent is

His followers include

He is best known for

I would believe it were true if

Name: _____ Date: _____

Legends
and the Supernatural

The legend I have chosen is

The supernatural character is

The main actions he/she performs are

I think these add to the story by

Without the supernatural elements, the legend's main events would be

Name: _____   Date: _____

A Modern Legend

This is the legend of   who is
dedicated to

               is supported by a brilliant band of companions

including   , who

and   , who

not forgetting   , who

The greatest adventure they have had so far happened
when

It's hard to believe but

In the end,

Name:_____   Date: _____

Features of Fables

The word fable comes from the Latin word **fabula**, meaning story.

Fables often have animals in them and usually teach a moral lesson.

Aesop's Fables are probably the most well-known.

Think about fables you know.

Fable	Animal Characters	Moral Lesson
The Tortoise and the Hare		

Name: _____   Date: _____

104

Retelling a Fable

Many fables involve trickery or foolishness.

The fable I have chosen to retell is

There were once

declared

But it didn't turn out that way

And the moral of the story is

Name: _____   Date: _____

Features of Science Fiction Stories

I know a story is about science fiction when

There are themes in science fiction which keep appearing. This chart shows some themes and books which reflect them.

Theme	Book	Author
Aliens		
Distant galaxies		
Experiments		
Technological change		

Many science fiction stories are set in the present, such as

Some are set in the future, for example

Others are set in the past, such as

Name: _____   Date: _____

Comparing Two
Science Fiction Classics

A Wrinkle in Time was written by Madeleine L'Engle in

20,000 Leagues Under the Sea was written by Jules Verne in

These stories can be called science fiction because

There are a number of similarities. Among them

The main differences between the two are

If I could change the ending of one of the stories, I would

Name:_____   Date: _____

Features of Adventure Stories

Adventure stories usually contain people who do not know what is about to happen to them.

Think of a place

at home	in the woods
in the park	on a train
at school	on vacation
at the sports center	in a shop

It was an ordinary Saturday morning and I was

Think of an incident

heard a...	saw a...
noise	smelled a...
scream	felt a...
shout	

I was thinking about

When, all of a sudden,

I decided to

Name: _____   Date: _____

A Great Adventure

An adventure story I enjoyed was
by

The reason I enjoyed it is

The most exciting part was when

The characters were interesting because

My favorite was

because

Name: _____ Date: _____

Writing a Mystery Story

Mystery stories are about mysteries to be solved.

Think of a mystery

| Lost person |
| Lost item |
| Buried treasure |
| A disappearance |

Think of characters in the story and the roles they will play.

Character	Role

Who will investigate the mystery?

What might happen to them?

How will the mystery be solved?

Use these notes to write your story on the back of this sheet.

Name: _____   Date: _____

A Major Mystery

A mystery story I know is called

Setting the scene

The story took place in

Identifying the characters

The people involved were

The mystery arises

No one could understand why

The plot thickens

What was even more mysterious was

Solution

It would appear that

Name: _____   Date: _____

Historical Stories

Historical stories are written about real events and are based on what happened. The author adds creative details to make the story more interesting.

An example is:

Story	Real Event	Creative Addition
Alfred the Great	Defeated in battle.	Burned the cakes while in hiding.

Think of a famous historical story you know and try to divide fact from fiction.

A story I know is

I think the event that really happened was

I think this because

I think the fictional addition to the story is

because

Name: _____ Date: _____

Historical Stories: Leaders

This is the story of _____ , who lived in

became leader when

Her/his greatest achievement was

I think the leadership qualities shown include

There are fictional elements to the story, such as

_____

Name: _____   Date: _____

Victory and Defeat

I have chosen the story of
to highlight the difference between victory and defeat.

The conflict was about

It lasted

The victory was achieved when

The effects on the defeated were

But the victors

Name: _____ Date: _____

A Sense of Time

Stories with an historical setting have to create a sense of the time in which the story is set. For example, a story about Christopher Columbus should not include detail about what was on TV at the time.

I have chosen the book
to examine a sense of time.

The plot

The language of the characters

Descriptions of place

The everyday items people use

Name: _____   Date: _____

Features of Classic Stories

Some stories remain popular for centuries because of the writer's skills. Sometimes, the storyline (plot) appeals to readers in each age — such as Hans Christian Andersen's **The Ugly Duckling**. Sometimes, the character, place descriptions and plot are brilliant, for example in Charles Dickens' writing. The beauty of the language, as well as character and plot, can also result in a classic — Shakespeare is an example.

A Christmas Carol

The storyline of **A Christmas Carol** tells of

The key character we dislike is
We dislike him because

The key character we pity and like is
He

I have selected this short description as an example of the qualities of Dickens' writing because

Name: _____   Date: _____

116

The Ugly Duckling

The **Ugly Duckling** is a classic tale because it touches our feelings.

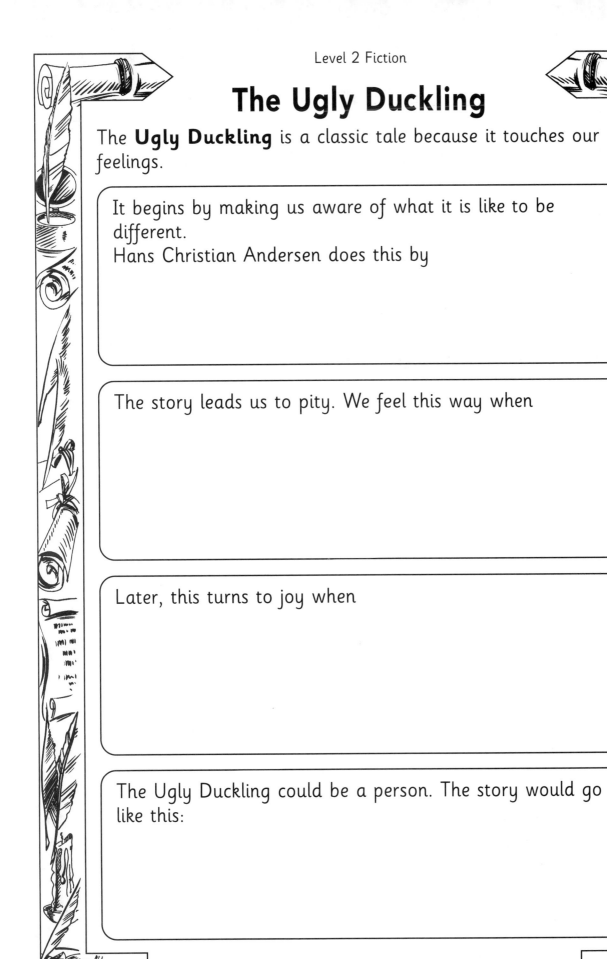

It begins by making us aware of what it is like to be different.
Hans Christian Andersen does this by

The story leads us to pity. We feel this way when

Later, this turns to joy when

The Ugly Duckling could be a person. The story would go like this:

Name: _____   Date: _____

Charles Dickens

This is an extract from a character description of
by Charles Dickens,
taken from his novel,

This is my description of
which I have written in the style of Dickens.

,

Name: _____   Date: _____

Shakespeare

Shakespeare often uses rhyming couplets for the dialogue of his characters. Here is an example from _____ , which is part of a speech by _____ to _____ .

This is my speech in rhyming couplets. The setting is a dialogue between _____ and _____ .

Name: _____   Date: _____

Plays: Setting

The play I am reading is called

The playwright is

The play takes place

The key features of the place are

The author has created a mood of

I think this place is interesting because

Another place that might also have worked for this story is

Name: _____   Date: _____

Plays: Characters

Play Title:

Playwright:

Name of Character:

Age and Appearance:

Personality (good and bad points):

Relationship to other characters in the play:

Key things this character says or does in the play:

Name: _____   Date: _____

Plays: Arguments
For and Against

A good example of a play where people have different points of view is

The two characters who disagree are

_____ argues   _____argues

_____   _____

_____   _____

because _____   because _____

_____   _____

_____   _____

The reasons they think this are

_____   _____

_____   _____

_____   _____

I think

because

Name: _____   Date: _____

Plays: Chronology

Play Title:

Playwright:

Use this timeline to make notes of the sequence of events that happen in the play.

Beginning

Conclusion

Name: _____   Date: _____

Non-Fiction: Genre

The term **genre** is used to describe the style or type of text or book.
Examples of non-fiction genre are:

autobiographies	information Books	reports
biographies	instructions	thesauruses
dictionaries	letters	timetables
directories	newspapers	
encyclopedias	recipes	

Write what genre each type of text is in the table below.

Book or Text	Genre
A book about planets	
A sports report	
Yellow pages	
A book written by a famous actor about his life	
A leaflet which tells you the times of trains	
A pen pal email	

Name: _____ Date: _____

124

Information Books

Information books normally have a contents page and an index. They are based on fact and usually do not tell a story. They are classified under a subject heading, such as science or history. Many contain photographs and illustrations.

Complete the chart, listing six books from the library.

Title	Classification	Contents ☑	Index ☑	Text ☑	Illus. ☑

Comment in detail on one of the books under each of the following headings.

Accuracy of contents/index:

Quality of text:

Value of illustrations:

Name: _____   Date: _____

Comparing Two
Information Books

The two books I have chosen are   and

. They provide information about

In terms of readability, I think

because

I prefer the illustrations in   , because

I found it easier to use the   in

Overall,

Name: _____   Date: _____

Outline Plan for an Information Book on My School

Chapter titles:

The main ideas I want to convey include:

-
-
-

Key words in the index:

Name: _____ Date: _____

My School

The school is situated

The subjects we study

The arrangements for lunch are

The school facilities include

The number of pupils in the school is
They are divided

Name: _____   Date: _____

My Favorite Team

The team I support is

They play at   , which is

A typical crowd for a home game is

The club was founded in   . It began

The players I most admire are

The reason I think they are special is

Name: _____   Date: _____

Dictionary Review

The dictionary I have chosen to review is

It was published by   in

I think the word list is

I was surprised not to find

There are appendices on

These are

The overall design of the dictionary is

My advice to someone considering buying this dictionary is

Name: Date:

Thesaurus Review

The thesaurus I have chosen to review was published by

in

It contains   headwords.

On average, there are   synonyms for each entry.

Some synonyms surprise me, for example

There are some synonyms which have not been included.
One I would have chosen is

The thesaurus has a number of other features, such as

I have compared it to the   thesaurus
and I feel that

Name: _____   Date: _____

Instructions: Live to be 100

Follow these instructions carefully and you should live to be 100.

1.

2.

3.

4.

5.

6.

7.

8.

9.

10.

Name: _____   Date: _____

Instructions for Using an Encyclopedia

In the library you will find the encyclopedia.

It is in   volumes.

To find information on a broad subject, you

For example, to find out about Brazil, you

To find information about a specific subject, you

For example, to find out about the London Underground, you

Name:_____   Date: _____

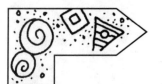

Persuasion

Dear   ,

I am writing to try to persuade you to

I think the main reasons you have not agreed so far are

but I think you are wrong.

First,

Second,

Finally,

Just think how much better it would be if you

you could

and

I really think you should reconsider and

Yours

To My Elected Official

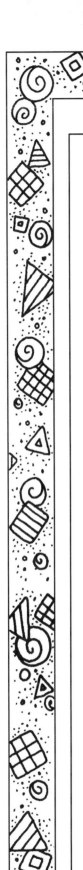

Dear   ,

As my representative, I want to write to you about

I feel the law should be changed because

I know that those who want to keep the present law will argue that

but I believe

Please do

Yours

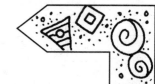

My Town

Dear   ,

I am writing to you in your position in the planning department.

I want to see this town improved and I suggest that

If this were to happen, then

and

Unless this happens, I believe

In conclusion,

Yours

Give It Up

Dear   ,

I am writing this letter to plead with you to change your lifestyle. I am, of course, referring to

If you carry on like this,

If you change now then the future will be different. You will

Don't just think about yourself but

One last time, I ask you

Yours

Complaint

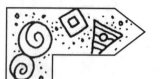

Ref:

Dear   ,

I am writing to complain about

which

I have since discovered that

I would be grateful if you would tell me what you propose to do about it.

If I am not satisfied, I will

Yours

Inquiry

Dear   ,

I am writing to inquire whether

I am actually looking for

I need the following features. It should

If you can meet my request, would you please

I look forward to hearing from you.

Yours

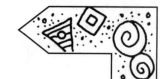

Explanation

Dear   ,

I am writing to apologize for

and to explain why it happened.

It all began when

I can honestly say that

Once it happened, I felt

I hope that having read my explanation, you

I promise that in the future

Yours

Recount

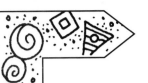

Dear   ,

I am writing to tell you about my most embarrassing moment.

It all began when

That led to

Imagine how I felt when

In the end,

My advice to others is

Yours

Congratulations

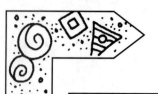

Dear   ,

I am writing to congratulate you on

I was so delighted when I heard from

What I most admire about your success is

I hope that in the future

Yours

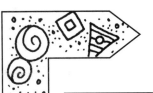

School Rules

Dear   ,

I am writing to try to persuade you to change the school rules.

The ones I am most concerned with are

My main objectives are

I am sure you think

but

Yours

Don't Miss the School Fair

Place: _____

Date: _____

Time: _____

You will see _____

_____

_____

You will be able to _____

_____

_____

_____

The special event will be _____

_____

_____

Name: _____ Date: _____

Subscribe to the Monthly School Magazine

Features	Benefits to you
Written by children for children	_____
List of local events	_____
Jokes	_____
Reviews of latest software	_____
Book reviews	_____
Upcoming events	_____

Only _____ each month.

Name: _____ Date: _____

Win a
Vacation to Disneyland

Answer the following questions correctly.

1. What is Disney's famous mouse called?

   _____

2. What is the name of the place where you can find Disneyland?

   _____

3. What was Disney's first name?

   _____

Write in no more than 15 words why you should win this trip.

Complete the form.

Name:

Age:

Address:

Zip Code:

Name: _____   Date: _____

Children's TV Critic Needed

The ideal child will be _____ years old.

A good critic will possess the following skills:

-
-
-
-

and will be interested in:

-
-
-
-

The successful person will be able to write

Name: _____   Date: _____

Recipe for a Healthy Life

A healthy person is one who

Healthy people do not

Activities that encourage healthy bodies include

Foods that are healthy include

And don't forget

Name:_____ Date: _____

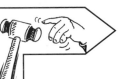

Child Labor

Pro: Children should be made to work from the age of six. Why should the rest of us work to keep children who do nothing but go to school and play?

Con:

Pro: Children are perfect for some jobs: cleaning under beds; as jockeys; testing cat and dog doors; sweeping old chimneys. Their size makes them ideal for such jobs.

Con:

Pro: By employing children, we can reduce costs. Children will work for low wages—even for sweets or videos. Then we could make bigger profits.

Con:

Having considered the pros and cons, I think

Name: _____   Date: _____

The Superiority of Men

Pro:

Con: On the contrary, just because in the past most presidents have been men is no proof of their superiority. Women didn't have the vote until much later than men and prejudice always lasts a long time.

Pro:

Con: It is simply not true that all great writers have been men. In modern times best selling authors include J. K. Rowling and Beverly Cleary. Laura Ingalls Wilder, Eve Bunting and Jane Yolen have also shown that women can be just as popular as men at writing.

Pro:

Con: I disagree completely. Women live longer than men. They keep their hair when men go bald. They don't complain when they are ill and most of them go to work AND run a home!

Name: _____ Date: _____

150

For the Motion

My friends, before us today we have the motion that

It should be obvious to everyone that

If that were not enough, I can add

Finally,

In conclusion, friends, I urge you to vote FOR the motion that

Name: _____   Date: _____

Against the Motion

We have listened to the arguments from   in support of the motion. I feel those arguments are wrong.

First,   told us

but I would say

Second,   argued

However, in my view

Let me now add a fresh argument of my own.

There is no doubt in my mind that we should oppose the motion that

And I urge you to vote against it.

Name: _____   Date: _____

Report on the Debate

A debate took place on   at

The motion before the house was that

____ spoke for the motion. The main points were

____ spoke against the motion and argued that

Comments from the floor included

The final vote was

Therefore, the motion was

Name: _____   Date: _____

A Life Story

The subject of the biography is

was born in

in the year

In early life,

is most famous for

This came about

In my opinion,

Name:_____ Date: _____

154

My Life

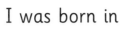

I was born in   in the year

The most interesting event of my early life was when

At the age of   , I

Probably the worst thing that has happened to me is

In recent times, I have begun

In the future, I hope

Name:_____   Date: _____

My Travels

Date: _____ Destination: _____

I left   at

on my journey to

The journey itself took   and the most noteworthy

event was

Once there, I stayed at   , which is

The highlight of my stay was when

During the stay, I also

Before I left, I

Name:_____   Date: _____

Remembering

My favorite anecdote about a member of the family concerns

The event took place at   in
and involved

As far as I know, what happened was that

Whenever we talk about this at home,

Name: _____   Date: _____

Diary Entry

Date: November 3, 1942

Another day wondering if the bombers will be over tonight.

As I walked along the street after dark, I noticed

and

It has to be like this because

Inside the house

Name: _____   Date: _____

Sick Report

Date: _____

This journal entry records what happened when I was taken ill with

I first knew something was wrong when

The symptoms were

The cure for this is

So I

At the worst point, I felt

I knew I was getting better when

My advice to others is

Name: _____   Date: _____

News Report

These basic notes arrived in my newsdesk office this morning. I have to prepare a newspaper report, complete with headline, in the next 20 minutes.

- new disease identified
- cure just discovered—standing on head and blowing bubbles
- slowly eats away the body
- starts at the toes
- local man has itchy big toe
- origin is unknown
- probably caused by watching boring TV
- warnings needed

Name: _____   Date: _____

Key Points

You are to give a talk to the class based on this text. You can make and use only eight short notes. Make sure your notes are clear and are about the main points.

We have been south and suffered a great deal there. Many have died of diseases which we have no name for. Our hearts looked and longed for this land where we were born. There are only a few of us left, and we only wanted a little ground, where we could live. I rode out and told the troops that we did not want to fight; we only wanted to go north, and if they would let us alone we would kill no one. My brother, Dull Knife, took one-half of the band and surrendered near Fort Robinson. They gave up their guns and then the whites killed them all.

I have heard that you intend to settle us on a reservation near the mountains. I don't want to settle. I love to roam over the prairies. There I feel free and happy, but when we settle down we grow pale and die. A long time ago this land belonged to our fathers; but when I go up the river I see camps of soldiers on its banks. These soldiers cut down my timber; they kill my buffalo; and when I see that, my heart feels like bursting; I feel sorry.

-
-
-
-
-
-
-
-

Name: _____   Date: _____

Message in a Bottle

You are trapped on a desert island. You have only the small piece of paper shown below. You will write a message on it and put it in a bottle. The message should contain brief notes which will help you to be rescued.

Name: _____   Date: _____

Observing

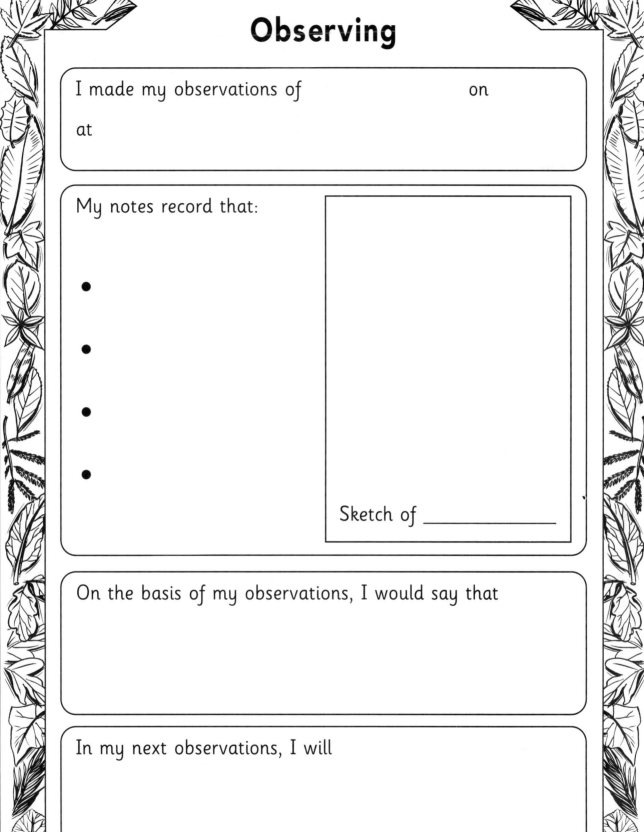

I made my observations of   on

at

My notes record that:

-
-
-
-

Sketch of _____

On the basis of my observations, I would say that

In my next observations, I will

Name: _____   Date: _____

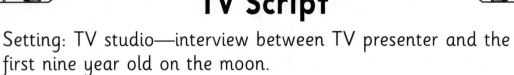

TV Script

Setting: TV studio—interview between TV presenter and the first nine year old on the moon.

Presenter: Ladies and gentlemen, with us today we have
who

Now tell us

Child:

Presenter: But surely your parents

Child:

Presenter:

Child:

Presenter: Let me thank you for

Name:_____   Date: _____

My Investigation Plan

I am planning to investigate

To help my investigation, I will need

The two most important questions I want to find answers to are

and

I expect to discover that

Name: _____   Date: _____

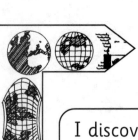

Investigation Report

I discovered that

What surprised me most was

I was really glad I

because

If I were to carry out another investigation, I would not

Name: _____   Date: _____

Observations

The geographical feature I observed was

I did this as part of my work on

The equipment I found really helpful was

The most interesting thing I learned was

I think this is because

My observations will help me to

Name: _____ Date: _____

Recording Evidence

Place visited:

Date:

My sketch of   shows

The notes I took show

I brought back with me

This is useful because

Name:_____   Date: _____

Drawing Conclusions

The evidence I have collected consists of

The most important evidence tells me that

In the light of my evidence, I believe that

I am not sure about

To be more certain, I will need to

Name: _____ Date: _____

Fieldwork Planner

I am planning a field trip to

I already know that

I will take the following items of equipment with me:
-
-
-
-

I will wear

because

I really want to find out

Name: _____   Date: _____

170

Field Notes

The first activity is

The most important point to remember is

At the second stop, I

I paid particular attention to

The equipment I have found most helpful is

Name: _____   Date: _____

Fieldwork Recount

During the fieldwork visit to ,
I learned that

I also learned

What surprised me most about the place was

I really enjoyed the part of the day when

I am still not sure

Name: _____   Date: _____

Making Maps and Plans

I have produced a map of
This is part of my work on

To find the information I needed for my map, I

I chose this scale because

The symbols I have used are

The key will help others to

Name: _____   Date: _____

Using Maps and Globes

I use a map to:
-
-
-

The map I am using shows

It is drawn to a scale of

The symbols which are most helpful to me are:

-
-
-

because

The most important thing I have learned from this map is

Name: _____   Date: _____

Describing a Journey

The journey I have planned is from

to

We will pass through

Between   and

we will see

The most interesting feature is

because

A good place to stop might be

because

Name:_____   Date:_____

Sources

In my study of _____, I have chosen to use

_____ as one of my sources.

It provides me with

However, it does not help me to

To find out more I would need to

Name: _____   Date: _____

176

Aerial Photographs

I have been using aerial photographs as part of my study of

The main human features shown are:

-
-
-

The main physical features I can see are:

-
-
-

The evidence tells me

I now need to look at a map to find out

Name: _____   Date: _____

Photographs

In the photographs of   I can see

I can also see

In addition,

What the photographs do not tell me is

To find this out I will need

Name: _____   Date: _____

Asking Questions

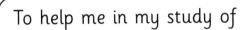

To help me in my study of

I need to ask a number of questions.

To find out about the jobs people do, I will ask:

-
-
-

To find out the environmental issues that affect people, I will ask:

-
-
-

To discover if local people would like their neighborhood to change, I need to ask:

-
-
-

Name: _____   Date: _____

Directions

My directions are from   to

Start by traveling in a   direction.

At this point,

You will now have reached
You should

When you arrive, you will see

Name: _____   Date: _____

Geographical Vocabulary

In my study of
I will try to use the following vocabulary.

Physical Features

-
-
-
-
-

Cultural Terms

-
-
-
-
-

Political Issues

-
-
-
-
-

Additional Vocabulary

-
-
-
-
-

Name: _____   Date: _____

Physical Features

The physical feature I am studying is

It is located

Sketch of _____

The effects of this feature on people are

Name: _____   Date: _____

The Seven Wonders
of the Ancient World

The Ancient Wonder I am studying is

It is located

Labeled diagram of _____

The main effect of this feature was

This wonder was built to

Name: _____   Date: _____

Changes from the Past

I have been studying changes in

The main sources of evidence I have used are:

-
-
-

The features that have changed the most are

The features that have stayed the same are

I prefer

because

I believe   could be improved

Name:_____   Date: _____

184

Changes Planned

I am investigating changes planned in

At present, the

The plan is for

The main reasons for the change are

I think the changes that should be made are

because

Name: _____   Date: _____

An Area in the World

The area I have chosen is

It has the following features:

-
-
-

There are some goods and services not available here.

These include:

-
-
-

To obtain these I would need to travel to

The main features of   are:

-
-
-

Name: _____   Date: _____

People at Work

In my town, _____, these jobs are important:

-
-
-

In the past, the most important jobs were:

-
-
-

The main reason these jobs are available here is

In the future, I think

Name: _____   Date: _____

Transportation

In _____, the main forms of transport are:

-
-
-

This is because

The main problems local people have with transportation are

I think transportation could be improved if

Name: _____   Date: _____

Leisure

The city of _____ , has these leisure features:

-
-
-

The first is located here because

The second

The area would be improved for leisure if

Name: _____   Date: _____

Making Comparisons

Similarities between _____ and _____ are:

-
-
-

Differences include:

-
-
-

The main factors affecting similarity and difference are:

-
-
-

Name: _____ Date: _____

190

Local Weather

I am studying the weather in

The rainfall pattern for the year shows that:

In spring,

In summer,

In autumn,

In winter,

The temperature pattern for the year shows that:

In spring,

In summer,

In autumn,

In winter,

The weather in this locality affects people's lives in these ways:

-
-
-
-

Name: _____   Date: _____

Comparing Weather

When I compare the weather in   with that in

, I find

They are similar in that in both

For example,

However, they are different in that

For example,

The differences in the weather are caused by

Name:_____   Date:_____

My Weather Forecast

My weather forecast, based on the past records of typical weather at this time of year, is

My weather forecast, based on the weather of the past three days, is

My weather forecast, based on data of conditions elsewhere and weather movement, is

Name: _____   Date: _____

Parts of a River

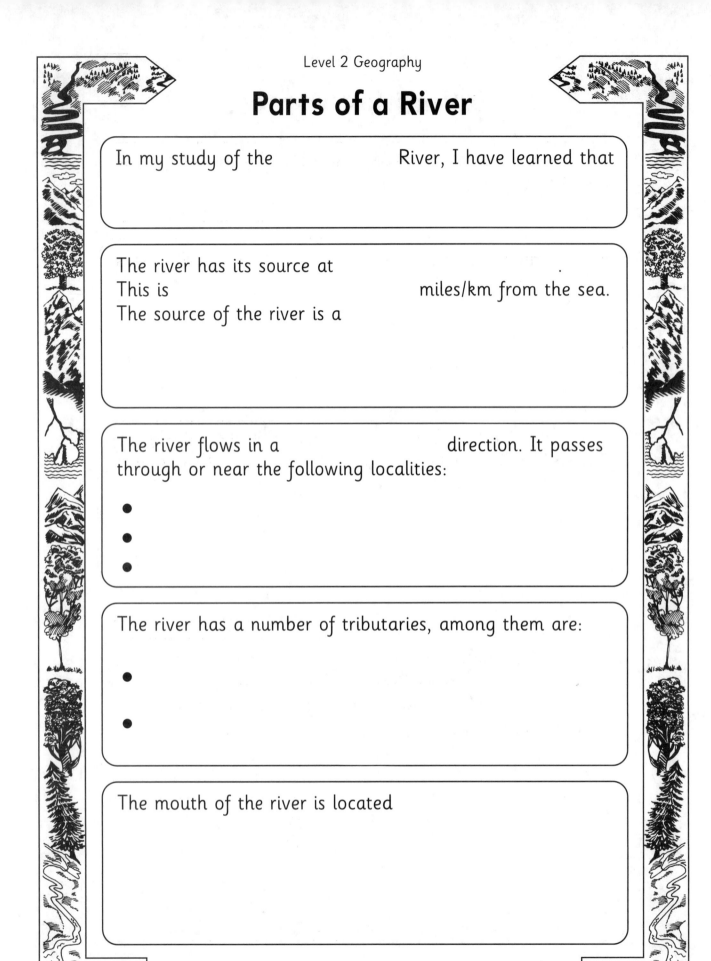

In my study of the _____ River, I have learned that

The river has its source at _____ .
This is _____ miles/km from the sea.
The source of the river is a

The river flows in a _____ direction. It passes through or near the following localities:

-
-
-

The river has a number of tributaries, among them are:

-
-

The mouth of the river is located

Name: _____   Date: _____

194

River Movements

The   River passes through different landscapes
as it flows from   to

In its early stages, the river is   . It passes
through land which is

The river is at its widest at   . At this point, I
would describe the landscape as

The most dramatic feature of the river is the   at
                    . This is caused by

In the future, I predict that the river will

Name:_____   Date: _____

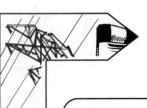

Comparing Regions

The two regions I am comparing are
and

The main features of   are

The main features of   are

Similarities between the two regions include:

-
-
-

Among the differences are:

-
-
-

Name:_____   Date: _____

Original Colonies

My chosen colony is

The name means

The first settlers were from

The main physical features of the colony were

The first products of this colony included

The main reason this settlement grew here is probably

Name:_____   Date: _____

Housing Patterns

In   , housing has these features:

-
-
-

Most of the houses are made from

This is because

The following types of homes are found in the area. I have listed them, starting with the most common:

-
-
-

The house types include

The best thing about the housing is

What I would most like to change is

Name:_____   Date: _____

Industry

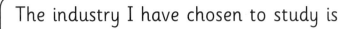

The industry I have chosen to study is

I know it is important in this area because

The reason the industry is located here is

If this industry were to move away or close there would be the following effects:

-
-
-

Name: _____   Date: _____

Conflict

There is a conflict because

One point of view is

On the other hand,

I would suggest

because

Environmental Change

The change that is planned is

The advantages are

However, the disadvantages are

Most people want

because

I think what should be done is

because

Environmental Concerns

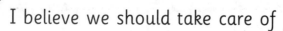

I believe we should take care of

The first point I want to make is

My evidence for saying this is

Second,

The evidence

In conclusion,

Name: _____   Date: _____

Special Environments

This environment is special because

If it is not protected

The greatest threat is

I believe we should

We need the help of

Name: _____ Date: _____

#3263 Writing Prompts and Models

Ecology

As part of a study of environmental problems, I have drawn up a plan to care for our planet.

There are these points to follow:

-
-
-
-
-
-

If everyone follows my plan, I believe

Name: _____   Date: _____

Chronology: Time Line

Start date

End date

My timeline begins in   and ends in

The three most important events in the period were:

-
-
-

Things might have been very different if

Name: _____   Date: _____

Chronology: Events

The events I studied happened in

The first important event was

Later,

Finally,

The events were important because

Name: _____   Date: _____

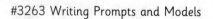

Chronology: People

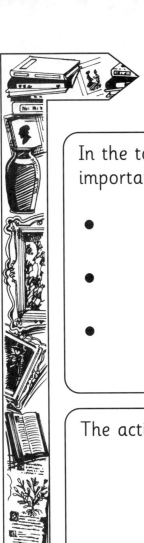

In the topic I have chosen, the following people were important:

-

-

-

The actions of   began events by

Later,

Finally,

Name: _____   Date: _____

Key People

A key person I am studying is

This person is most famous for

Other things   did include

My opinion of   is that

Name: _____ Date: _____

Key Events

Key events I have studied are

What happened before the key events was that

Immediately after the key events,

As a result of all this,

Name: _____   Date: _____

How We See The Past

The particular events I have studied are

These events have been viewed differently by different people.

Some people thought

Others, however, thought

My view is that

Name: _____   Date: _____

Our Opinions
Can Be Different

The event I have chosen to report on is

In the past, people have believed that

They reached this opinion because

My view is that

I have reached this conclusion because

Name:    Date: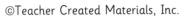

Historical Inquiry

I am planning to investigate

To help my inquiry I will use the following sources:

-
-
-
-

The two most important questions I want to find answers to are:

and

I expect my inquiry will lead to the opinion that

Name: _____   Date: _____

Using Written Sources

The written source I have chosen is

It was originally produced in

My copy is

The main facts I have learned from this source are

and

What the source does not tell me is

The main advantage of a written source is

Name: _____ Date: _____

Using Artifacts

The artifact I am studying is

Its date is

Labeled diagram of _____

This artifact was used

I know this because

The most important thing it tells me about the period is

Name: _____   Date: _____

Using Pictures and Paintings

The picture I am studying is

It was produced in

In its original form, the materials used were

My example is from

The three most important points I have learned from the picture are:

-
-
-

We have to be careful when using picture evidence because

Name: _____ Date: _____

Using Photographs

The photograph I am using was taken in

It shows

The photographer was probably

What the photograph does not help me understand is

Name: _____   Date: _____

216

Buildings

The building I am using as a source is

It was built in

Labeled sketch of _____

The materials used tell me that

The design of the building makes me think that

Name: _____ Date: _____

Oral Evidence

I listened to oral evidence from

The four most interesting events I heard described were:

-
-
-
-

I thought the evidence was most reliable on

However, I thought it less reliable on

The greatest strength of oral evidence is

Its greatest weakness, however, is

Name: _____ Date: _____

Posing Questions

To help me in my study of
I need to pose a number of questions.

To find out about the personal life of the person, I will ask three questions:

-

-

-

To discover what they know about the events I am most interested in, I will ask,

Name: _____   Date: _____

Note-taking

I am making notes on   because

The most important point I have noted is

In addition, I note that

What this tells me about the period I am studying is

My next step is to find out more about

because

Name: _____   Date: _____

Fieldwork

We went on a visit to   as part
of our study of

I produced this labeled sketch of the site.

The most important feature I saw was

because

In its original state, the site would have had a number of
differences including

Name:_____   Date: _____

Fieldwork Follow-up

When I consider what I saw on my visit to
I have learned that

I now need to find out more about

In order to do this, I will

This should help me discover

Name:_____ Date: _____

222 ©Teacher Created Materials, Inc.

Using the Internet

I used the Internet to find out about

The best site I found was
I learned that

Other useful sites were

The most important things I learned from these were

A site I would recommend is
because

Name: _____ Date: _____

From the Internet

I used the Internet to help me in a study of

I have downloaded an image of
from site

I have selected and edited the following text from the Internet.

Name: _____   Date: _____

224

Sources and Change

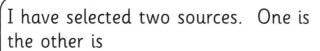

I have selected two sources. One is   ,
the other is

The first choice is dated   and the second
source

The changes I can see by comparing the two sources include

I think these changes happened because

The sources are similar in a number of ways

Name: _____   Date: _____

Family Tree

I have produced the family tree of

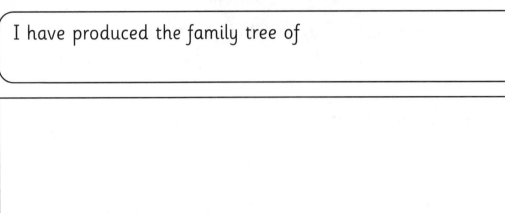

I have learned that _____ 's father

and that _____ 's mother

The most famous ancestor was _____ , who was
famous for

Name: _____ Date: _____

226 ©Teacher Created Materials, Inc.

Political Events

I have been studying

The most powerful people at this time were:

-

-

-

They were in control because

As a result of what they did,

Name: _____   Date: _____

Economic Events

I have been studying

During this period, trade

This was because

The most important goods traded were:

-
-
-

These were important because

Most trade was between

because

Name: _____   Date: _____

228

Scientific and Technological Events

I have been studying

The three most important scientific and technological changes in the period were:

-
-
-

The reason these changes happened is

I think the biggest change to the lives of the people would have been

because

Name: _____ Date: _____

Social Events

I have been studying

The three most interesting things I have learned about the lives of the people are:

-
-
-

In my opinion, the biggest change in social life was

It came about because

The difference it made to the people was

Name: _____   Date: _____

230

Religious Events

I have been studying

In this period, most people believed that

They worshipped

Religious buildings were

The most common evidence from the period is

The main difference between then and now is

Name: _____   Date: _____

Culture

I have been studying

Most people spoke

The most interesting written source I know about from this period is

It was produced

It is special because

The most popular pastime enjoyed by the people was

A toy I have seen evidence of was

Name: _____   Date: _____

Art and Artists

I have been studying

My favorite piece of art or sculpture from this period is

It was produced at , in
by

I think it is excellent because

People at the time would have liked it because

To see it today, you would need to go to

Name: _____ Date: _____

Explorers' Motives

I have been studying the

I think there are three main reasons why these people came to the United States

-
-
-

Of these the most important is

because

The most important legacy from these times is

My evidence for this is

Name: _____ Date: _____

The Presidents

In my opinion, the greatest president was

I believe this for three reasons:

-
-
-

I think the high point of the administration was when

However, the low point was

The greatest legacy left for us was

Name: _____   Date: _____

Health

In _____ times, many illnesses were common including

I think the worst was _____ . The symptoms were

and the treatment was

I believe the greatest improvement in public health was

What happened was

Since then,

Name:_____   Date: _____

Changes in Leisure: 1950-Today

This chart shows the five most popular leisure activities for children in my class.

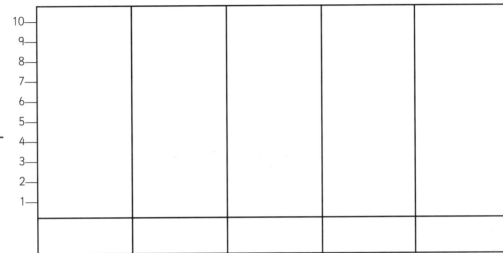

Hours per week

10
9
8
7
6
5
4
3
2
1

Activity

In the 1950s, most children spent their leisure time on

I know this because

The reasons for the differences are

My favorite activity is

because

Name: _____   Date: _____

Myths and Legends of Ancient Greece

My favorite story from the Ancient Greeks is

It tells of

I know it is true/not true because

The reason it is still popular today is

I have re-written the story for the 21st century. Allow me to introduce a very modern hero

Name: _____   Date: _____

The Legacy of Ancient Greece

This chart shows a list of English words which have Greek origins.

English	Greek	Meaning

My favorite building, designed in the style of the Ancient Greeks, is

It was built in

The two main types of columns in Greek architecture are

The Olympic Games began in

The first events included

Pythagoras was born circa 580 BC. He is credited with

Name: _____   Date: _____

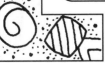

Ancient Egypt:
Death and Beyond

The Ancient Egyptians believed that when a person died,

We know they believed this because

In order to make a successful journey to the afterlife, many preparations were needed. Among them were

Most of our evidence is about rich and powerful people. This is because

Name:_____ Date: _____

Local Study: Origins

My town is called

The word means   and it has this name because

The first time   was referred to in a
written document was

This chart shows the changes in population of the locality.

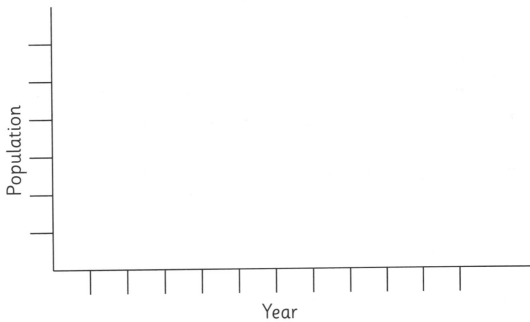

As you can see,

Name: _____   Date: _____

Journal Writing Prompts

After school I like to…

Sometimes I am sad because…

 My favorite book is about…

The first movie I ever saw was about…

 When I grow up I will…

I wonder what it would be like to be a…

 If I was a bird I would…

I am happy when I can…

Paragraph Topics

Write about a favorite stuffed animal.

 Write about things in nature that you like.

Write about what you like to eat for lunch.

Write about a favorite thing to do on a Saturday.

Write about a dream you had.

Write about what you want to be when you grow up.

 Write about why you like recess.

Write about what to do when it's raining.

Story Writing Prompts

Write a different ending or beginning for a favorite story.

Write a fairy tale in which your best friend is a character.

 Write a silly story about a little pig.

Write about a place where everything is the color green.

Write a story about a teacher who whispered everything.

 Pretend you are an ice-cream cone.

Pretend you are a tree. Write about who lives in you.

Write about a magic potion. What does it do?

244

Character Sketch Prompts

Describe the oldest member of your family. Mention something this person taught you.

Create a super hero. Describe how he or she looks, what he or she wears and what makes a hero.

Describe a villain. Mention characteristics. Describe where the villain lives. Describe how he or she looks.

Imagine the pet you always wanted. Describe how it looks and what you would do together.

Describe your ideal best friend. Use at least five different adjectives.

Describe a character in a book you like. List as many details as you can.

Improving Verb Usage Prompts

Assign one or more of the following activities to give students practice using well-chosen verbs. Remind them that verbs add power to their writing by creating action in the reader's mind.

The Playground

Draw a picture of your dream playground. Then, write five sentences containing strong verbs about what happens at the playground. To create a challenge, each verb can only be used once. To use technology, word process the sentences and highlight the action words in different colors. Create a bulletin board of dream playgrounds and sentences containing vivid verbs.

The Kitchen

As a class, brainstorm a list of appliances and gadgets found in the kitchen. For each object, think of at least one action verb the particular appliance, gadget, or tool has the ability to do. Choose three objects and illustrate them in action. Finally, brainstorm five action verbs for one of the illustrated objects.

I Said, You Said

The word "said" is overused, especially when writing dialogue. As a class, brainstorm a bulletin board of verbs showing the many ways words can be spoken. Write a dialogue between two or three people. See how many words from the list you can use instead of the word "said."

246

Descriptive Writing Prompts

Meet My Friend

Everyone has a best friend who is unlike anyone else. Think about your best friend and his or her qualities, such as she makes you laugh or he listens to your problems.

Write an essay to explain why this person is your best friend. Include examples and details to describe this person's personality.

Character Sketch

Sit in a location where you won't be noticed. Study the appearance and actions of a person you can see. Notice the following: the physical appearance of the person, how the person is dressed, how the person's face and hair looks, what the person is doing, and what the person might be saying or thinking.

Write a character sketch of the person you have been studying. Try to capture the "essence" of that person's character. Be sure to include specific details, using precise word choices.

Criminal Description

Pretend you have witnessed a crime and the police have asked you to describe the appearance of the criminal for their wanted poster. Think about the following aspects: what the criminal looked like (including the criminal's approximate age, height, and weight; facial features; hair color and style; distinguishing marks such as scars, tattoos, etc.), whether the criminal was male or female, and what the criminal was wearing.

Write a paragraph for the police, describing the appearance of the criminal for their wanted poster. Be sure to include specific details, using precise word choices.

Descriptive Writing Prompts *(cont.)*

My Favorite Room

Write a narrative paragraph describing your favorite room in detail. Next, tell what you enjoy doing in this room.

The Perfect Vacation

Describe your ideal vacation spot. First, brainstorm what makes a great vacation. Draw your vacation spot. In one narrative paragraph, tell why this place is the ideal vacation destination.

I Have to Go Where?

Make a list of all the places you don't like to go, with reasons why. Choose one of these awful places and compose a narrative paragraph revealing why this place is not high on your "fun-places-to-visit" list.

Games People Play

Describe a sports setting: stadium, diamond, rink, arena, garden, auditorium, etc. Explain not only what it looks like, but also what type of sport is played there. This description and explanation should be addressed to someone who has just arrived on Earth.

Descriptive Writing Prompts *(cont.)*

Babysitter Report

Pretend you are babysitting for two wild, out-of-control children. You know their parents are going to ask you how they behaved. You don't really want to tell the parents how bad the children were because you want to seem in control of the situation, but you don't want to lie to the parents either.

Think about how you can describe the children's behavior by "cushioning" your words a little. Think about what the children did and what they said. Decide how you can describe the children "softly" to their parents. Be sure to include specific details, using precise word choices.

Scientifically Speaking

Think about a particularly interesting science experiment you've conducted. Every experiment has a purpose, procedures, and a conclusion based upon the data. Explain your favorite experiment from start to finish. Then include a graph of the data you collected, or draw a picture of the procedures or conclusion to help explain what you did.

On the Playground

What new playground equipment would you buy if you had $5,000 to spend? Write a letter persuading your principal new equipment is needed. Perhaps you have some new equipment in mind, or perhaps you would like to see an old piece of equipment replaced.

Make a map of the playground. Use symbols to show the locations of the equipment. Make a map key. Include the new equipment in your map. Then write a letter to your principal explaining why this equipment should be purchased.

Persuasive Writing Prompts

Current Events

Read an article about a recent or past event that encourages disagreement over an issue. Write a one-or two-sentence summary. Think about the two sides of the story and decide with whom you agree. Write a paragraph to try to persuade others to agree with your viewpoint. Design a poster to visually explain your opinion.

The Best Thanksgiving Dinner Ever

Most people can't imagine being anywhere else for Thanksgiving other than where they usually go. Think about where you spend your Thanksgiving holiday and the luscious foods you enjoy. Try to persuade a classmate that your grandma, mom, aunt, dad, or cousin is the best Thanksgiving cook around.

The Reluctant Leprechaun

Leprechauns are supposed to show you where they've hidden their pot of gold—if you can ever catch one. But what if you did and he refused? How would you persuade a leprechaun to take you to his pot of gold? Think of some ideas explaining to this uncooperative leprechaun why you deserve the pot of gold.

Adventure Story Starters

Story Starter

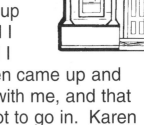

Sam shouted loudly so that I could hear. He yelled that he thought I was a chicken for not wanting to go into the haunted house. Sam went on in and began climbing up the broken staircase. I came to the doorway and said I thought the stairs were going to break. Sam just said I was afraid of ghosts and haunted houses. Then Karen came up and tried to get me to go in. She said that she would go with me, and that way Sam wouldn't think I was a chicken. I decided not to go in. Karen went on in to follow Sam. I sat and waited for over half an hour. Suddenly…

Story Starter

The noontime blast of the firehouse siren announced the start of the town's bike race. For months, Meg had been practicing. She wanted to win first prize. The first place winner got a brand new ten-speed bike. At first, the hours of practice seemed to pay off as she sped ahead of all the other bikers. Then, from out of nowhere, George whizzed past. There were only a few laps to go when…

Story Starter

Martha and Kathryn had been hiking all day in the woods. Now they were miles from nowhere. The sun was starting to set, and Martha suggested that they head back. Kathryn agreed that it was a good idea.
The girls looked around for some trail markers. They couldn't find any. "Oh, no!" said Martha, "We're lost! And we don't even have a flashlight!"

Adventure Story Starters *(cont.)*

Story Starter

Kristen ran into the stable and threw her arms around Ginger. Ginger was Kristen's very own horse. "They can't sell you," sobbed Kristen. She clung to Ginger's mane and stroked it gently. She cried over and over again. All of a sudden, she jumped on Ginger's back and they raced out of the stable.

Story Starter

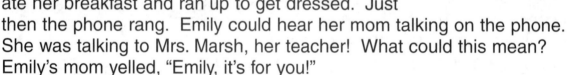

Emily jumped out of bed and quickly put on her robe. She ran down the stairs in such a hurry! Was she going to be late on the first day of school? She was so nervous about going into second grade. She had heard that mean Mary was going to be in her class. She was scared of her. Emily ate her breakfast and ran up to get dressed. Just then the phone rang. Emily could hear her mom talking on the phone. She was talking to Mrs. Marsh, her teacher! What could this mean? Emily's mom yelled, "Emily, it's for you!"

Story Starter

The snake came slithering out of its cage. Not one of the students in Mr. Schmidt's class even noticed. Soon after the snake slithered off the counter, the lunch bell rang. All of the students ran to get their lunches and then lined up at the door. When the bell rang again for the students to come back from recess, they opened the door. Anne was the first one back to her seat. Suddenly, she screamed.

Letter Writing Prompts

Beautifying the School Grounds

Quick Write: Brainstorm ten things you could do to beautify your school grounds.

Write a letter to your principal describing your plan to beautify the school. Support your plan with at least three reasons. You might want to include a drawing of your proposed garden, landscaping ideas, and/or a budget for your project. In your reasons, you might consider benefits to the environment, desirability of the school to community members, and learning opportunities for other students in the school. Remember to develop your ideas fully and clearly and maintain a respectful tone.

Adding a Book Series to the School Library

Quick Write: List your favorite book series and/or five of your favorite authors.

Suppose you and your classmates want to add a new book series to the school library bookshelves. Write a letter to the librarian in which you present your request and at least three reasons why you think this book series would be a good addition to the library. You might want to include the entertainment value, the educational value, and the cost. Remember to develop your ideas fully and clearly and maintain a respectful tone.

Planning a Community Service Project

Quick Write: List five possible community service projects you could do.

Suppose you and your classmates have a great idea for a local community service project. Examples include the following: a community leaf rake, a trip to the soup kitchen, visiting the senior citizen's center, reading to the young children at the library, picking up trash in the local park, etc. Write a letter to your teacher describing the project. Include at least three reasons to support your request. In your letter, consider how this project will benefit the organization being served and the school community. Remember to develop your ideas fully and clearly and maintain a respectful but firm tone.

Letter Writing Prompts (cont.)

Adding a Snack Item to the Cafeteria Menu

Quick Write: List 10 of your favorite snack foods.

Suppose you and your classmates want to add a new snack item to the school cafeteria. Write a letter to the head cafeteria worker in which you clearly state your request and at least three reasons why you think this snack item would be beneficial to the cafeteria menu. You may want to include the nutritional benefits, cost, and taste of the snack item. Remember to develop your ideas fully and clearly and maintain a respectful tone.

Performing a Play

Quick Write: List three of your favorite plays. Next, list five topics for original plays.

Suppose you and your classmates want to perform a play after school for your friends, family, and local community members. Write a letter to your teacher in which you clearly state your request and at least three reasons why you want to perform this play. State the title of the play you are going to perform and the entertainment and educational value of the play, as well as the amount of money you could raise for the school by performing the play. Remember to develop your ideas fully and clearly and maintain a respectful tone towards the audience.

Requesting Team Uniforms

Quick Write: Design a logo for a team uniform.

Suppose your team does not have enough money to purchase team uniforms. Write a letter to a local business requesting sponsorship of the uniforms. Be sure to describe your team to the business by including the sport that you play and the age and gender of the players. Then, include the reasons that this business should sponsor the uniforms. In your letter, consider the positive publicity for the business and the positive value of supporting local athletes and schools. Remember to develop your ideas fully and clearly and maintain a respectful but firm tone.

Letter Writing Prompts *(cont.)*

Toothpaste Scenario

Suppose you bought some toothpaste last night at the store. The toothpaste, which was manufactured by the Sparkling White Toothpaste Company, was the same brand you always buy. You like this brand of toothpaste because it is the cheapest and prevents cavities. Later that same evening, you unscrewed the toothpaste lid and prepared to squeeze some toothpaste onto your toothbrush. But something didn't seem quite right. You looked closer, and you saw a hair sticking out of the toothpaste lid. Yuck! You decide to write a letter to the CEO of the company.

Cold Pizza Scenario

Suppose you went to a restaurant and ordered pizza. You waited over a half an hour for your pizza, and when it arrived, it was cold. You say something to your server, but she just shrugs her shoulders and says, "Oh well, that's what happens sometimes." You decide to write a letter to the manager of the restaurant to complain about the service you received.

Defective Model Car Scenario

Suppose you bought a model car at a local department store. When you got home, you opened the box and were surprised to discover that many of the car pieces were broken. You decide to write a letter to the manufacturer of the model car to complain about the product and to request that the manufacturer be more careful when shipping and handling merchandise.

Editorial Writing Prompts

Being Polite in the Local Movie Theater

Quick Write: Brainstorm three reasons why it is important to be polite in a movie theater.

Suppose you and your family recently went to see a movie at the local movie theater. While you were there, a number of other people in the theater were talking loudly and throwing popcorn during the movie. Write an editorial for your school newspaper in which you request that the members of your community be polite and respectful towards the other people in the theater by remaining quiet and refraining from throwing things. Clearly state your stance on this issue and include at least three reasons to support your request.

Removing Smoking Ads from Local Malls

Quick Write: List three reasons why smoking is bad for you.

Suppose you and your family were walking around the local mall on a Saturday night. You notice that there are some smoking ads posted outside the mall near the pay phones. Write an editorial for your school newspaper in which you request that the owner of the mall remove the ads. Clearly state your stance on this issue and include at least three reasons to support your request.

Being Quiet During a Fire Drill

Quick Write: Make a list of three things you have to do during a fire drill.

Suppose you and your classmates have to evacuate the school building during a routine fire drill. During the drill, you notice that your classmates are very noisy. Write an editorial for your school newspaper in which you request that your classmates be quiet and orderly during fire drills. Clearly state your opinion on this issue and include the following reasons for requesting a quiet, orderly fire drill: kids need to be able to hear their teachers' directions in order to be safe; older kids need to provide a good example to younger kids; and teachers will be impressed with the responsibility of quiet kids and give them more privileges.